D1605705

REAL MEN
Don't Say
Splendid

• *A Lexicon of Unmanliness* •

by Michael Gorman

PETER PAUPER PRESS, INC.
White Plains, New York

To my parents, to Katie,
and to Lori's husband, who thought
the Christmas party was delightful

THANK YOU

Designed by Heather Zschock

Copyright © 2007 Michael Gorman
Through arrangement with the Mendel Media Group LLC of New York

Published by Peter Pauper Press. Inc.
202 Mamaroneck Avenue
White Plains, NY 10601
All rights reserved
ISBN 978-1-59359-876-1
Printed in China
7 6 5 4 3 2 1

Visit us at www.peterpauper.com

REAL MEN Don't Say Splendid

• A Lexicon of Unmanliness •

lexicon ('leksu`kón) *noun*

A language user's knowledge of words—
vocabulary, mental lexicon

A reference book containing an alphabetical list
of words with information about them

unmanliness (ən-'man-lē-nəs) *noun*

The trait of being effeminate (derogatory
of a man)—sissiness, softness

Introduction

We all know instinctively that there are some words real men just shouldn't say, no matter what the circumstances—words that make a man seem a little less manly when he says them.

Call them words with nuance, or "feminine" words. Call them whatever.

Men, for example, should never refer to chit chat before they say bye-bye and skedaddle. They should not speak of *tinkle* in a bathroom context, nor express amazement with the word "*Golly.*"

Saying one of these words on a first date is relationship suicide. Women cringe inside when they hear a guy say these words and, just like that, the guy slips from "the man of my dreams" to "my good friend Steve, Tom, Dave…"

This book is a list of those words—99 of those words, to be exact. Accompanying each word is an example of the word's use. Understand that the example sentence provided is just that—an example. The word should not be used in any sentence at any time by a man ever. Men—especially those trying to attract positive female attention—should remove these words from their vocabulary, starting today. Even in today's world of feminists and men's groups, female bosses and stay-at-home dads, these are the words that pave the way to the land of never after.

So without further ado,
I present you with
REAL MEN DON'T SAY "SPLENDID":
A LEXICON OF UNMANLINESS.

ACCESSORIZE

That's a pretty dress.
How do you plan to
accessorize it?

ADORABLE

Oh, you should have seen it!
An **adorable** family of
bunnies hopped by.

Beige

Something in white
or BEIGE would go
well with those pants.

BLEMISH

I wish this blemish on
my face would go away.

Bliss

We had an evening of wine, dancing, and great conversation. It was pure BLISS.

BLOUSE

I don't remember that blouse.

Boobies

You know Cindy;
she has really big BOOBIES.

BOUTIQUE

Let's stop in some boutique
and find you a top for tonight.

Bye-bye

BYE-BYE!

CANOODLING

Nothing happened???
Puh-leeze, I saw you two
canoodling all night.

CAPTIVATING

Her smile was
captivating.

CHARMING

You gotta hand it to the guy.
He's got a **charming**
way about him.

Chic

Late night at the
Continental is the CHIC
scene on Saturday.

CHILLY

Oh, I'm just going to grab a jacket.
It's a bit **chilly** out here.

CHIT CHAT

Office chit chat is getting in the way of work.

Comfy

I want to wear something
COMFY for the hike.

Cuddle

I like to CUDDLE for
hours after sex.

Dainty

My wife's so dainty—
that's why I love her.

DANDY

Everything is just fine
and dandy.

Dashing

She looked dashing
in her red dress.

Dazzled

I was **dazzled** by the performance.

DELIGHTFUL

I regret not being able
to attend, but thank you for the
delightful invitation.

DERRIÈRE

Oh my God, I think
that woman just pinched
my derrière.

DILLY-DALLY

I want to get in and get out. I don't want to dilly-dally.

DIVINE

Her singing was divine.

Doily

The right DOILY under
that lamp would really
highlight its beauty.

ELEGANT

The bride's dress
was elegant.

ENSEMBLE

Every member of the
cast is a star. This is a
true ensemble.

FABULOUS

Mary? Oh, I think Mary is fabulous.

Fancy

Say what you will,
but I enjoy **FANCY** things.

FAUX PAS

I may have made a slight faux pas when I forgot to bring a gift to the party.

FEMININE

Let's just say she wasn't the most
feminine-looking thing.

FLUFFY

I need my pillows fluffy,
or I toss and turn all night.

FRAGRANCE

She was bewitching, and
the fragrance she
wore drew me in.

FROLIC

Sometimes we like to sit in the back yard and watch our dog, George, frolic in the grass.

Gaga

I went GAGA when
I heard the news.

Gala

It's going to be the GALA
of the century.

GALPAL

I read somewhere that Lenny Kravitz
was spotted walking around L.A.
with a new galpal.

Giggle

Every time you say that,
it makes me GIGGLE.

GLAMOROUS

I like a girl in false eyelashes.
They look so glamorous.

GLITZ

Hollywood is missing all the **glitz** and glamor
of the old days.

Golly

GOLLY, that is a lot of shrimp for one person!

Gosh

GOSH, I've never really thought about it that way.

HEART THROB

Is her husband still the **heart throb** he was ten years ago?

HEELS

She was wearing a halter top,
a short skirt, and a
pair of black heels.

Hunk

I'm no HUNK,
but I have been told I'm
a good-looking guy.

HUNKY-DORY

I'm doing just hunky-dory.
Thanks for asking.

Kitty-cat

Come here, KITTY-CAT, come here!

LINENS

Don't you love the smell
of fresh linens coming
out of the dryer?

LIP-LOCK

It started off as innocent flirting,
but it turned into a
full-on lip-lock.

LOVELY

Everything was *lovely*,
from the dress to the
ceremony to the reception.

MINGLE

I found myself standing
in one spot all night and never
really got the chance to walk
around and mingle.

No-No

Honey, that's a NO-NO.
We don't do that here.

NUPTIALS

And should we expect to see you at the nuptials?

Oops

Oops!

OUTFIT

Is that new? I've never seen you wear that outfit before.

PANTIES

Do you have any
panties for me to throw
into this load of laundry?

PASTELS

Let's stick to dark colors,
and avoid pastels
in this room.

Peachy (KEEN)

I thought I'd be hungover
this morning, but I'm
feeling PEACHY.

PERIWINKLE

I love my warm periwinkle comforter.

PIZZAZZ

This song's really got
pizzazz!

POTPOURRI

An apple and cinnamon potpourri is just right for the kitchen.

PRECIOUS

I'm afraid to hold her,
she's just so precious.
Too precious!

PREGGERS

Guess who's preggers?

Pumps

Why don't you wear your white PUMPS with those pants?

Purse

Honey, would you please put
my keys in your PURSE?

RUFFLE

OK, maybe I was trying to **ruffle** some feathers.

Sashay

If the club is lame,
we'll just SASHAY our way
right out of there.

Sassy

Listen, don't take that
SASSY attitude with me!
It's not going to fly.

SAVOR

Hold on, hold on—
I just want to savor
this moment.

Scoot

Excuse me, do you think you
could SCOOT over a bit?

SCRUMPTIOUS

From the appetizers to the main course to the dessert, everything was truly scrumptious.

Sequin

She looked fantastic in that little SEQUIN number.

SHIMMY

My date is not a dancer,
but she has been known to do
a little shimmy from
time to time.

Sizzle

She SIZZLED in that dress.

SKEDADDLE

I wish I could stay,
but I must skedaddle.

Slacks

Honey, where are
my grey SLACKS?

SMIDGEN

I would like just a **smidgen** of parmesan on my spaghetti, please.

SNUGGLE

We sat there and snuggled
for quite a while, before it turned
into something more…
if you know what I mean.

SOIREE

We'll get some people
together and have ourselves a
soiree to celebrate.

SPECTACULAR

It was a truly spectacular
recital, and the diva's arias
were over the moon.

SPLENDID

We stayed at a splendid hotel, literally a block from the beach.

SPRITZER

You know what? I'll have a wine **spritzer**, please.

Tad

Just a TAD of black pepper please.
Just a TAD...

Tasty

Now that is one
TASTY sandwich.

TEENY

This **teeny** adjustment to my hair makes all the difference in the world.

TIDBIT

She forgot to tell me that little tidbit.

Tiff

I wouldn't say it was an all-out fight.
But yeah, we certainly
had a little TIFF.

TINKERBELL

My assistant is always looking out for me. He's my own little Tinkerbell.

TINKLE

Is there a bathroom around
here I can duck into
for a tinkle?

TIPPY-TOES

I still wasn't able to see
what was going on, even on
my tippy-toes.

Tipsy

Looks to me like someone
is a bit TIPSY.

Tizzy

I went into a complete TIZZY when I heard the news.

Tummy

It must have been something I ate,
because my TUMMY is
starting to ache.

Whisk

Let's WHISK you away
and get you a drink.

WHOOPSY-DAISY

Whoopsy-daisy!

Wiggle

Excuse me, do you mind if I
WIGGLE past to get to
the dessert table?

WILLY-NILLY

Instead of taking his time,
he sped willy-nilly
through it all.

Yummy

Mmmmm ... yummy!